Contents

Introduction

To walk into a decorator showhouse is to enter the realm of ideas, new ideas on products, styles, and colors fired by talented designers' inspirations, visions, and flights of fancy. Both the general public and professional designers alike receive insight walking through these amazing spaces.

Designer showhouses are open to the public largely during the spring and early summer months of April, May, and June. However, summer and fall showhouses are found in Northern states in the United States, while February finds showhouses ready to go in balmy Florida.

Multitudes of dedicated volunteers work with designers to make magic happen within the walls of a designer showhouse. Interiors of mostly historic homes are transformed and deadlines met to create the impression of serene and seamless beauty with no hint of the mad scramble of design and fabrication that occurred before the doors swung smoothly open on the first day. For weeks, crowds come and viewers are inspired and amazed by the transformations found in each and every room. Once the doors close for the final time, the interiors of the venerable home are returned to their previous state, donations are made to worthy hospitals and charities, and the show is done.

Captured here are the designs that came and went from a variety of showhouses. The purpose is to preserve those ephemeral masterpieces of interior design for all those who could not attend the original shows. The venue has changed, but the inspiration remains the same. So open the door and tour these transformed historical homes room by room.

Foyers & Hallways

Cosmopolitan Craftsman Holiday Entry

Sandpiper's Holiday Homes Tour
Sarah Barnard Design
Photographer: Scott Van Dyke

This Christmas tree was specially designed, based on the homeowner's architecture and love of the color blue.

Cosmopolitan Craftsman Foyer

Sandpiper's Holiday Homes Tour
Sarah Barnard Design
Lone Pine Pictures

The gorgeous chocolate brown foyer compliments the abundance of stone.

Fireside Foyer

Madame Walker Showhouse
George Bond Interior Designs
Photography by Marisa Pelligrini

An expansive greeting room is classically furnished, its coffered ceiling setting the stately tone.

Petite Retreat

Stately Homes by the Sea
Sheila Rich Interiors, LLC
Photography by John Martinelli

A cozy sanctuary greets visitors in this stately foyer. Exquisite ornamental bird-motif ironwork frames the room's arched window, underlined by a memorable settee.

Gardener's Grand Entry

Stately Homes Showhouse
Jim Dove of Canterbury Design Kitchen Interiors
Photography by Marisa Pelligrini

A foyer showcases a gardener's passion in a vaulted entry. The adjacent mudroom belies its name, adding elegance to the art of potting and efficiency to floral arranging.

Fairy Foyer

Twin Maples Showhouse
Sherrie Legro Round of Enchantment Lives
Photography by Marisa Pelligrini

Rustic elements, stone, marble mosaic, and fanciful furnishings set a tone of enchantment for this fairyland entry space.

Reflecting Space

Twin Maples Showhouse
David Peer of European Country Kitchens
Photography by Marisa Pelligrini

Mirrored cabinetry adds a sense of space to a narrow entryway; a mudroom that provides for tucked away storage of boots, coats, and umbrellas. Platforms and drawers slide out and transoms lift up to provide storage and seating for the comings and goings.

Foil to Femininity

Museums of Old York Designer Show House
Nicole Yee of NY Interiors
Photography by James R. Salomon and Jim LaBranche

A passageway provides a dressing area rich in natural light, where neutral black and whites provide a modest backdrop for selecting the evening's attire.

Studies & Libraries

The Library

Stately Homes by the Sea Designer Showhouse, Sheep's Run
Interior Design by Byford & Mills
Photography by Marisa Pelligrini

Leather bound housed in illuminated niches, the masculine and feminine play of chintz, plaid, and houndstooth as well as other paired textures and patterns converge to create an elegant yet casually warm space reminiscent of an English country library with a decidedly unconventional twist.

Literary Retreat

Stately Homes by the Sea
Russell Minion & Juan Carlow Gutierrez of Minion-Gutierrez
Photographer Peter Rymwid

Inspired by the work of twentieth century British architect Sir Edward Lutyens, the room comes to life with inviting textiles and muted wall colors. A wall of faux painted wood doors serves as a backdrop, enhanced by a south facing line of transom windows that filters the light and invites you into the space.

Office Space

34th Bucks County Designer House & Gardens
Kelley Price Interiors
Photographer: Katrina Mojzesz

A breathtaking landscape sets the stage for this His & Hers Office. Orange accents energize the space to create a productive environment.

blink
FREAKONOMICS

inspire.

Madame's Study

32nd Bucks County Designer House & Gardens
Phillip Greenberg, Kristin Crawford, & Elisabeth Steklis of Greenberg Interiors
Kim Billingsley Photography

A quiet study serves up a beautiful view, a place to gather thoughts and organize papers, and a lounge perfect for catching up with a good book.

Panel Decision

Birmingham Symphony Decorator Showhouse
Perry Umphrey ASID, RID of Umphrey Interiors
Sylvia Martin Photography

The paneled walls of this study were buffed with tung oil, and the room was infused with white elements to help counteract the dark effect of the wall-to-wall paneling. A new dimensional fireplace surround was built to effect glass brick.

Lofty Library

Birmingham Home & Garden Loft Tour
Perry Umphrey ASID, RID of Umphrey Interiors
Sylvia Martin Photography

Sheer curtains and Lucite® chairs add air and illumination to a library area with an incredible view of the city of Birmingham. A cowhide acts as an earthy anchor on the floor.

Studious Escape

34th Bucks County Designer House & Garden
Jere Bradwell of European Home Collection
Photography: Joy Levy

Mahogany and burl walnut on the Italian console and the unique oval partner's desk complement the chocolate wallpaper and rich wood paneled walls in this Country Gentleman's home office.

Office

Sandpiper's Holiday Homes Tour
Sarah Barnard Design
Scott Van Dyke

A hardworking office gets a luxurious makeover.

Living Rooms

Sun Spots

Birmingham Home & Garden Loft Tour
Perry Umphrey ASID, RID of Umphrey Interiors
Sylvia Martin Photography

Tangerine tones punctuate a great room, drawing attention to the curtains, footstools, and a specially commissioned painting so big it had to be brought through the window by a crane. A hammered bronze table creates a central core in this lofty, uplifting space.

New Life

Montgomery, Alabama Decorator's Showhouse
Perry Umphrey ASID, RID of Umphrey Interiors
Sylvia Martin Photographer

Contemporary furnishings and a hand blown chandelier add new life to this sister home to the governor's mansion. Keeping the lines clean accents the home's natural beauty but updates it for today's lifestyle.

Midcentury Manhattan

Kips Bay Showhouse
James Rixner of James Rixner Interiors
Photographer: Nick Johnson

This amazing room designed by James Rixner for the 2007 Kips Bay Decorator Showhouse was entitled "Midcentury Manhattan". Located on an upper floor of an Upper Eastside Townhouse, it boasted a full roof terrace, and a view down Fifth Avenue that included the Empire State Building, something very rare in a townhouse. The original access to the terrace was through a small set of stairs on the left side of the door. By expanding the stairs to the full width of the room, Mr. Rixner created a wide access to the terrace and a viewing platform. In addition, this dramatic focal point draws one's eye to the vintage Quan Yin sculpture which pervades the space with an elegant sense of serenity. This quintessentially Manhattan room features a smaller version of the Lobmyer chandelier that was installed in the Metropolitan Opera House. Other important design elements include the fireplace wall rendered in Rosewood, important artwork and sculptural upholstered pieces. The soothing palate of soft celadon and warm ivory serve as a backdrop for the rich wood, dramatic artwork, and the lime green draperies. White accents pieces complete the space and add the perfect dramatic touch. Contributors to the room included: carpeting by Stark; drapery fabric by Kravet; wall covering by Zoffany; sofa by Michael Berman; ottomans by Carole Gratale; slipper chair by Nancy Corzine; end tables by Alan Moss; and lamp by Porta Romana.

Living Room Detail

Sandpiper's Holiday Homes Tour
Sarah Barnard Design
Photographer: Scott Van Dyke and Lone Pine Pictures

The Arts & Crafts Style with a sophisticated and luxurious approach. In true Arts & Crafts tradition nearly every piece of furniture was custom made for this home. This unique environment is brimming with organic edgy-ness through the distressed floors and the custom commissioned artwork.

Formal Living Room a.k.a. Ballroom

Heritage Square Museum's Holiday Historic Home Tour
Sarah Barnard Design
Photographer: Brad Nicol

An original marble mantle piece and authentic Victorian antiques adorn this grand Italianate ballroom separated by pairs of Corinthian columns and delightfully dressed in shades of pink and green. The room also includes a truly Victorian holiday tree! Inspired by William Hayes Perry's involvement with the Rose Parade and illuminated with real wax candles.

Gleaming antique pine paneling, wide-planked pegged floors, walls upholstered in blue jacquard and trim create a stunning backdrop for this late 1920s country living room. A distinctive collection of fabrics, fine art, and treasured antiques create a warm & inviting glow in this grand room.

An Extraordinary Gathering

Stately Homes By The Sea, The Metcalf Estate
Interior Design by Byford & Mills
Photography by McKay Imaging

Living Elegance

32nd Bucks County Designer House & Gardens
Christie Meehan and Janet Plaza of Hendrixson's Furniture
Kim Billingsley Photography

A mix of English and American furnishings punctuate this comfortably sophisticated space, amidst a fresh spring palette of warm salmon tones with punches of caramel and robin's egg blue.

Living with Style

Vassar Showhouse & Gardens
Gloria Steward Lycknell Interiors
Photographer: Ann Stratton

We wanted a sense of style to drive the selection we made for this architecturally beautiful room. The space has become warm yet sophisticated, fashionable but homey, colorful though subtle in tones and complex despite being at ease with itself. All choices were made with a full awareness of the importance of scale, texture, and compatibility while creating a space where either one person or a group would feel comfortable.

Portrait Salon

34th Bucks County Designer House & Garden
Melinda Kuehne of Gracious Living
Kim Billingsley Photography and Melinda and Hal Kuehne

An elegant yet comfortable living room reinterprets an Old World concept in living. Authentic Venetian-plastered walls and ceiling act as foils to eglomise and gilded flourishes, while plush seating makes it easy to enjoy each detail.

DANCING

Sitting, Gathering, Keeping

Fair and Square

Nyack Showhouse, Nyack, New York
Ho Sang Shin of Antine Shin, LLC
Marisa Pelligrini Photographer

A series of squares reflect the room's focal point – big plate glass windows connect indoors with out in a fire-warmed sitting area. Exotic sculpture and wood elements bring warmth to crisp, contemporary white and aluminum furnishings.

Swirling Salon

Twin Maples Showhouse

Russell Minion & Juan Carlos Gutierrez of Minion-Gutierrez

Photography: Marisa Pelligrini and John Martinelli

A reinterpretation of an eighteenth century oval ceiling medallion in the Robert Adam's style sets the tone for a contemporary sitting room alive with movement and light. A gold etched mirror designed by Minion Gutierrez magnifies the light effects of a wealth of windows, framed in luxuriant textiles. Each piece of furniture was designed by the designers for this room, creating a space of peace and serenity for an imaginary traveler client.

Taste of the Orient

Designer Showhouse of New Jersey
Ho Sang Shin of Antine Shin, LLC
Marisa Pelligrini Photographer

Bright blues and whites unite a collection of unique lighting and ceramics, creating a contemporary nod to our ancestor's taste for refined Oriental imports. The walls have a washed finish, adding depth to the carefully orchestrated two-tone theme.

Solarium Imaginarium

The Designer Showhouse of New Jersey
Barbara Ostrom Associates
Photography by Marisa Pelligrini

Faux painting creates a window to the sky through the solid vaulted ceiling of a family sitting room. A federal-style mantel embraces a wide-screen for television viewing, while logs await a match below.

The Beauty Found in Nature

The Museums of Old York Decorator Show House
Boehm Graham Interior Design
Photography by Terry Welch

While sitting and sipping cognac with friends, our curiosity is piqued as we investigate the natural history on display. This is natural beauty at its best, reminiscent of the curiosity cabinets first seen in the homes of royalty and the aristocracy in sixteenth century Europe. Collections acted as both workshops and libraries for all to enjoy. White linen fabric, a steer-hide rug, a shark jaw, a beaver skull, a framed African stick bug, natural woodwork, and white birch logs echo the simplicity of Nature. Candlelight, fireplace warmth, and reflected daylight add a layer of coziness to this inviting space. Crisp and fresh, simple and well edited, white lacquered walls are juxtaposed by the warm natural tones of the woodwork. A pair of floor mirrors reflects light and expands the space visually. The oil paintings and accessories highlight the beauty and symmetry found in unexpected places in nature.

Provencal Enchantment

32nd Bucks County Designer House & Gardens
Pierre Deux French Country
Kim Billingsley Photography

Inspired by the French countryside, this room revels in the sunny colors and sentimental textiles of one of Europe's most inspiring spots – the area of Provence.

Sunny Sitting

34th Bucks County Designer House & Garden
Chris Robinson of Chris' Cottage
Kim Billingsley Photography

Yellow adds cheer to a warm, earthy sitting room, with cocoa walls and soft settees.

Evening Retreat

32nd Bucks County Designer House & Gardens
Rita Myer of Becoming Home Design
Kim Billingsley Photography

A sanctuary at the end of the day, this room offers up a comforting palette of robin's egg blue and soft mocha, with soft cuddle chairs for reading bedtime stories by the fire.

A Serene Salon

DogHaus Designer Showhouse
Carrie Leskowitz Interiors
Photography by John Armich

Just a note of crimson and a slight blush overhead breath life into an elegantly furnished room.

Gathering Room

32nd Bucks County Designer House & Gardens
Patricia Childs of Village Flower Shoppe, Ltd., Haute House Interiors
Kim Billingsley Photography

A comfortable family area is created using rich colors found in the farmhouse's landscape.

Family Room

Sandpiper's Holiday Homes Tour
Sarah Barnard Design
Photographer: Charlie Daniels

The modern luxury of this patio level family room reflects the individuality and youth of the homeowners. Wall hung guitars reflect the homeowners' love for music and personal style. A display of one of a kind pieces: an antique brass lamp and a hand carved mahogany conch shell from Negril.

Backyard Patio

Sandpiper's Holiday Homes Tour
Sarah Barnard Design
Photographer: Charlie Daniels

A cozy patio pairs luxurious outdoor textiles with Chinese artisan pottery to create a quiet retreat.

Sun Streaked

Twin Maples Showhouse
Rachel Kapner of Creative Interiors
Photography by Marisa Pelligrini

Pink stripes underline a sunny space outlined in pretty paned windows. A thick raffia fabric in a coral tone finishes the wall, highlighting the whimsical paisley and embroidered sheer fabrics that adorn the windows. Furnishings and textiles bring an Asian flair while accenting the cherry blossom tones of a fanciful, cheerful place.

The Loggia

Stately Homes by the Sea Designer Showhouse, Sheep's Run
Pat Mills and Robin Gilbert of Byford & Mills
Photography by Marisa Pelligrini

A boxwood and ivy trimmed outdoor living area is an ideal retreat and the perfect spot to gaze upon the beautifully appointed grounds. The striped portieres soften and anchor the space.

Kitchens

Tuxedo Kitchen

The Museums of Old York Decorator Show House
Boehm Graham Interior Design
Photography by Terry Welch

The turn of the century "Vanity Fair" gentlemen prints set the tone for a fun, elegant, and dramatic men's-club-inspired gourmet kitchen. As the eighteenth century naturalist Comte de Buffon suggests, "Le style est l'homme meme"—The style is the man. This man-inspired kitchen, with its suiting fabric, a gold gothic chandelier, black "suede" walls, gold crest buttons lining the draperies, and the bar seat caps resemble a man's dress shirt.

Kitchen Classic

Alabama ASID

Betsy Keller, ASID, of Red Door Interiors

Photography by Jeff White

A soothing palette straight from the garden graces a sophisticated country kitchen.

Country Kitchen

34th Bucks County Designer House & Gardens
Mary Catalino of Doylestown Kitchen and Decorating Studio, LLC
Kim Billingsley Photography

The craftsmanship of Amish-built cabinetry is combined with comfortable seating and country elements to warm a contemporary kitchen fired by state-of-the-art appliances.

Fancy Pantry

Twin Maples Showhouse
Jim Dove of Canterbury Design Kitchen Interiors
Photography by Marisa Pelligrini

A gilded ceiling helps illuminate a butler's pantry, a bonus room that was doubly blessed with double-hung window and plumbing.

Dining Rooms

Vaulted Feast

Susan G. Komen Holiday House Designer Show House
Charles Pavarini III Design Associates, Inc.
Photography: Daniel Eifert

A festive dining room marries sophistication with drama. The design had to live up to the raw materials: a tremendous 32 x 20 foot room with a 14-foot high barrel vaulted ceiling with antique plaster mouldings, and a stone colonnade on the south elevation leading to a sculpture garden. The decorations, complete with scenic murals and period antiques, reflect a passion for living with an exuberant fall color scheme, contemporary art, and massive-scale table-scape.

A Room For All Occasions

Mansion in May, The Cross Estate
Interior Design by Byford & Mills
Photography by Marisa Pelligrini

This room provides the perfect place in which to gather family and dear friends and one's favorite collections; a room that is well suited for a formal celebratory dinner as it is for a leisurely breakfast or a late night game of backgammon. - OR - A space commonly considered the most formal and seldom used room in a home is transformed into a warm and inviting dining and living area suitable for all occasions.

Expansive Seating

Stately Homes by the Sea
Luis Acevedo Interior Design
Photography by Peter Rymwid

An eclectic collection of English and French pieces in rich dark mahogany woods and light painted finishes are set against a light and airy backdrop of cream painted paneling and a custom-printed Chinese wallpaper in celery greens. The ceiling was painted in a soft coral shade that changes with the light throughout the day and gives the space a warm glow at night.

Euro Fare

32nd Bucks County Designer House & Gardens
Jere Bradwell of European Home Collection
Photography: Joy Levy

Classic Scalamandre fabrics, and a hand-crafted Harvest table from Habersham, set the stage for an elegant country dinner party in this lovely old dining room on the estate of Earl Jamison, founder of Peddler's Village in Lahaska, Pennsylvania. The classic wing back chairs for host and hostess give a regal effect to the table setting. Beautiful Italian ceramic accent pieces and a hand-painted chandelier from Bradburn gallery complete the room.

Indigo Coast

34th Bucks County Designer House & Garden
Mary Stein and Tracy Mancini of Hunting and Gatherings
Kim Billingsley Photography

A dining room evokes the British Colonial era, weaving together textures of indigo sea grass, ancient parchment, tortoised bamboo, and gilt.

Dining Room

Heritage Square Museum's Holiday Historic Home Tour
Sarah Barnard Design
Photographer: Brad Nicol

A vignette is set with blue toile-like chairs arranged by a built-in cabinet, while a peacock graces the dining room's Christmas tree.

Dining Room

Sandpiper's Holiday Homes Tour
Sarah Barnard Design
Scott Van Dyke

The dining room features a hand painted mural inspired by the California Live Oak Tree.

Coastal Elegance

Museums of Old York Showhouse 2010
Nicole Yee, Owner NY Interiors
Photography by Greg West

This inviting dining room is richly layered with neutral tones and textures. Deep grey walls, light linens, and a creamy gloss ceiling conjure seaside images of glistening salt spray and sandy beaches. The original art over the fireplace makes the neutral room come alive with brilliant blues. Tall French wingbacks create drama as the head chairs. A floor-length table cloth sets off white placesettings, vintage linens, and striking blue glassware. Natural textures that make the room feel beachy and comfortable are balanced with glamorous touches such as the high-shine ceiling, delicate crystal chandelier, and classic mirrors. The overall result is a stunning room that guests will enjoy in comfort. Beautiful in its simplicity, this room is fresh and fabulous.

Bedrooms

Yin Inn

Southwest Florida Symphony Show House
Kira Krümm Interior Design
Randall Perry Photography

Silver capiz shells found on the beach established the aesthetic concept for this room, executed in shades of grey and metallics such as pewter and silver. A careful study in balance, this room was crafted to embody the characteristics of "Yin," or the feminine, soft and restful, diffused and tranquil.

Beyond the Bed

Kips Bay Decorator Showhouse
Charles Pavarini III Design Associates, Inc.
Photography: Daniel Eifert

The renaissance bedchamber is modernized, brought forward in a more livable manner. The furnishings are more useable, and there is function there with a desk area, a dressing area, and a sitting area. The diaphanous, hand-embroidered draperies partially obscure the bed, evoking passion and romance.

Sunlit Suite

Nyack Showhouse, Nyack, New York
Ho Sang Shin of Antine Shin, LLC
Marisa Pelligrini Photographer

An open four-poster bed doubles as deep seating in a sun-soaked sunroom that also serves as an inviting guest suite.

Sleeping in Symmetry

Mansion in May

Rachel Kapner of Creative Interiors

Photographer: David Groul

Cheerful sunshine-toned walls are echoed in a mirrored sculpture rising behind the royally appointed bed. Two love seats and lamps flank a folding screen, forming a perfectly paired sitting area atop a cushy shag carpet.

Isadora's Dream

Mansions in May

Nina Karamallis and the Design Team of British Home Emporium

Photography by Marisa Pelligrini

Handmade Italian embroidered lace drapery, feminine fabrics, and peach tones create a dreamlike setting that invites retreat both day and night. A mirrored vanity is positioned for maximum views of the pastoral scene outside.

Old Fashioned Contemporary

34th Bucks County Designer House & Gardens
Tom Gass of Gass Design
Photography by Peter Paige

A dancing figure adds an essence of celebration to the marital suite. Contemporary lines belie the antique-like elements of his and hers silhouettes and bedside furnishings.

Soft Squares

ASID Designer Showhouse / Women's Guild of the Huntsville Museum of Art
Suzanne Richard Barnes of Richard & Company Interior Design
Photographer: Jeffrey J. Hanshaw

Textiles and thick carpeting provide a sense of sinking in within an environment tied together by repeating brown squares in pillows, furnishings, and floral art.

Rustic Guest Retreat

34th Bucks County Designer House & Gardens
Greg and Sue Evans of Tuscan Hills, LLC
Kim Billingsley Photography

The colors of Tuscany warm a welcoming guest house, including fabric designs and handcrafted furniture and accessories from Italy set amidst textured walls finished with marmorino plaster, an ancient Italian technique that utilizes marble dust.

Restorative Retreat

32nd Bucks County Designer House & Gardens
Gloria Steward Lycknell of Lycknell Interiors
Kim Billingsley Photography

The interests and tastes of the occupants are reflected in the soft surroundings, where attention to detail, and efficiency in the furnishings makes this a special room of solitude, rest, and rejuvenation.

Modest Elegance

34th Bucks County Designer House & Garden
Melinda Shorday of All the Trimmings
Top Kat Photography Inc.

I always think of a room as an autobiography. What does my client want in their journal, their scrapbook? It should be a reflection of their past, their present, their future dreams. When I create a room for a designer house, I "create" a client for the space before I begin the design. For this room my "client" was a young couple on a tight budget who wanted a fresh and comfortable space that incorporated less than perfect family hand-me-downs.

Moderation rules the space with a focus on comfort without excess. Living green includes reusing old family pieces, found items, and antique linens. The distressed leather chair is the only "new" piece in the space, with all other items receiving updates through a touch of paint or new handles. The quilt top, a flea market find, was machine quilted and paired with crisp new hotel-style linens. The "splurge" in the room is the Brunschwig & Fils fabric used on the gathered bed skirt and the stunning custom hanging lights. The sophisticated paisley updates the vintage pieces and provides the palette for the space.

I love to use local art, photography, and personal artifacts to give character to a room. In this case we used photography from favorite local sites the "clients" like to visit along with framed character playing cards from childhood. Simple window treatments echoing the paisley's colors, a slip-covered parson's chair, and grandmother's suitcases stacked as a side table all contribute to a room full of personality, color, and comfort created with budget in mind.

Dream Days

Twin Maples Showhouse
Katja van der Loo of Papyrus Home Design
Photography by Marisa Pelligrini

Art finds its niche in a dayroom dedicated to its display. A bed serves guests, but also acts as a platform from which to enjoy treasured objects.

Sunshine Guest Room by the Sea

The Museums of Old York Decorator Show House
Boehm Graham Interior Design
Photography by Terry Welch

A guest's perfect retreat is created in this bedroom drenched in sunshine and cooled by the ocean's breeze. Antique Redote Hummingbird prints wrap the room. The sharp contrast of the black accents keep it fresh and current while the seagrass, straw hats, and baskets provide a casual, yet sophisticated retreat for reading, relaxing, and dreaming of days gone by and days to come. The toile headboard and Frette linens invite any tired beachgoer.

Craftsman Style Guest Room

Cape May Show House
Michele and Bill Collins, Painted River Studios
Photography by John Armich

True to craftsman style but updated for modern living. This bedroom with a hand-painted mural should please the most finicky guest.

Pretty in Pink

Alabama ASID
Betsy Keller, ASID, of Red Door Interiors
Photography by Jeff White

Yellow and green team up with accents of pink for a feminine retreat, made more romantic through a wealth of draping textiles.

Guest Bedroom

Sandpiper's Holiday Homes Tour
Sarah Barnard Design
Photographer: Charlie Daniels

An innovative guest room features a custom bed with metallic leather headboard and a claw foot base.

Second Guest Bedroom

Sandpiper's Holiday Homes Tour
Sarah Barnard Design
Photographer: Charlie Daniels

A painstakingly veneered custom headboard features a floating desk drawer and a vintage 1930s office chair that melds Hollywood Glamour with Industrial Chic.

Eave's Ease

Twin Maples Showhouse
Caitlin Rutkay of C.R. Interiors Designs
Photography by Marisa Pelligrini

Tucked into a cozy nook of the roofline, this attic retreat offers a roost-like retreat.

Her Room … a retreat from a snoring husband

Twin Maples Showhouse
Ashley Moos Interiors
Photography by Marisa Pelligrini

Leopard skin underlines a woman's retreat, boldly surrounded in walls of the most feminine hue. Chinese porcelain and a vintage Murano chandelier add sky blue tones to a daring attic retreat clearly staked out for her leisurely repasts. The daybed is a nineteenth century Meridienne from a New Orleans dealer. The lamps are Christopher Sptizmiller, the side tables Vaughn Designs, the pink wall silks and hydrangea fabric are from Clarence House and my workroom Stessl & Neugebauer. The custom linens are Matouk from A HOME.

Attic Attraction

Twin Maples Showhouse
Kim Nadel of Niche
Marisa Pelligrini Photographer

A lofty space gains allure, with panels that warm the walls and complement the wooden structure supporting the home's roof. Comfy, eco-friendly furnishings can be quickly rearranged on the tatami mats to accommodate small groups or large, or make room for overnight guests.

Children's Bedrooms

Nostalgic Nursery

ASID Designer Showhouse / Women's Guild of the Huntsville Museum of Art
Audra Kennedy Designs, LLC
Photography by Jeff White

The owners of the 100-year-old farmhouse where this event was held have a little girl, and the nursery was designed with her in mind. An artist's hand created the cloud-painted ceiling and the little birds and animals that await discovery on the walls. The bedding and valances are hand embroidered with silk ribbon.

New Royalty

33rd Bucks County Designer House & Gardens
Cindy Brody of Le Blue Goose
Kim Billingsley Photography

The room was designed as a nursery on the third floor of a beautiful farm house. The third floor ceilings were very low and I decided to do the tent motif to give height to the low windows and walls. I decided to do a girls room with the tent design to make it fun, but also a sophisticated circus theme. The shades were hand painted with circus animals taken from the crib bedding. We mounted the shades higher on the wall to give the room a little lift. I used a white shag carpet on the floor that would be great for a baby or for a little girl to play house with her little friends. The room was done in soft taupe and pale pinks and white. It was a quiet room with lots of interesting features and a pleasure to do.

Elementary Environment

Mansion in May
Rachel Kapner of Creative Interiors
Photographer: David Groul

Minty pastel creates a peaceful respite for both mother and child. The wallpaper softly repeats a pastel stag motif, and other forest creatures populate the space in plush forms.

Sailor's Loft

32nd Bucks County Designer House & Gardens
Lisa Cicalese McMillen of Cica Lisa Designs
Photographer: Katrina Mojzesz

A lofty boy's quarters evoke a shipboard cabin. Decorative painter Lisa Cicalese McMillen sailed with this idea, creating a hand-painted nautical chart on the slanted ceiling, and washing the walls in a faux finish reminiscent of sea and sky.

1743 FB

The sails we see on the ocean
Are as white as white can be;
But never one in the harbor
As white as the sails at sea
Carlotta Perry
heaves, the ship swings free The sails swell full To sea, to sea!
Thomas Lovell Beddoes

Little Man's Room

Sandpiper's Holiday Homes Tour
Sarah Barnard Design
Photographers: Charlie Daniels; Sarah Barnard

A boy's bedroom is transformed into a "little man's" room with traditional warmth and cutting edge details to create a youthful, contemporary space. A wall mural featuring a vintage Aston Martin is inspired by the classic James Bond movie Goldfinger.

JB007

ZOO

Girl's Room

Sandpiper's Holiday Homes Tour
Sarah Barnard Design
Photographers: Charlie Daniels; Renee Fox

The antique painted beds are a traditional foundation, while the light fixture and custom glass bubble mural creates a playful harmony. Playful bubble art made of recycled crushed glass adds whimsy to this little girl's room.

Kids' Craft

34th Bucks County Designer House & Gardens
Joan L. Curtis, Designer & Muralist
Kim Billingsley Photography

A children's studio nurtures budding artists, inspiring them, and their parents, to be creative. A chalkboard wall, easels, art materials, and some artwork all get the creative juices flowing.

Bathrooms

Miss Pew's Recession Retreat

34th Bucks County Designer House and Gardens, 2009
Tom Gass, Gass Design
Peter Paige Photography

The ladies' side of the outhouse is done in original, tasteful Pepto Bismol pink and recession blue. It features a crystal chandelier and a gilded framed portrait of Miss Pew (by the designer) showing an expression of disdain.

Pewter Powder

Twin Maples Showhouse
Jonathan Hress
Photography by Marisa Pelligrini

A black and white palette creates a contemporary powder room space. A beautiful valance frames the gossamer-clad window, fanned by hand-painted features on matching walls.

Gilded Corner

Huntsville Museum of Art's Designer Showhouse
Suzanne Richard Barnes of Richard & Company Interior Design
Jeff White Photography

Reminiscent of the old adage, this powder room boasts of something old, something new, something borrowed, and something ... sapphire blue. Keeping the fabulous formal black and white octagon tile floor the room came with, the designer added a new sink and granite, borrowed some local artwork, and hung draperies of pewter and sapphire silk.

Powder Room

Sandpiper's Holiday Homes Tour
Sarah Barnard Design
Photographer: Scott Van Dyke

A powder room inspired by nature with a custom Arts & Crafts mural.

Opulent Water Closet

33rd Bucks County Designer House & Gardens
Amanda Bertele of Superior Woodcraft
Kim Billingsley Photography

A custom vanity with book matched burl and exotic stone resides in this petite powder room where the designer, partnering with Wendy Kleiner of HighFire Designs and Kelly Willard of Schlichter Tile & Marble Contractors, created a dramatic floor of celadon tile set in Roussillon red grout.

Powder in the Jungle
Twin Maples Showhouse
Alice Shanahan Interiors
Marisa Pelligrini Photographer

Red zebra stripes and a faux leopard skin create a petite jungle, making a powder break a memorable event.

Textured Toilette

Southwest Florida Symphony Show House
Kira Krümm Interior Design
Randall Perry Photography

Beehive and pebble textures bring a natural feel to a honey-toned monochromatic bath.

Perfect Powder

Twin Maples Showhouse
Shannon Hall of Shannon Hall Designs
Photographer: Marisa Pellegrini

A two-tone motif keeps it simple in a tidy powder room, where the barest hint of sky blue color shines within the basic contrasts of warm brown wood tones and crisp ivory tiles.

Master Bath

Polo Master Builders Showhouse
Shannon Hall of Shannon Hall Designs
Peter Rymwid Photography

A spacious, cool, and revitalizing modern master bath with rustic elements paired with details echoing the Victorian age. This bath won third place in the National Kitchen and Bath Association's 2009 competition, category seven, large baths. The bath's components are: fittings by Perrins and Rowe, soak tub and room accessories by Waterworks, Jerusalem Bone limestone and Verde slate mosaic floor, Verde Reale polished countertop, Quoizel pendant, Crackle tiles by Quemerc, and distinctive painted and stained oak cabinets by Peter Solerno, NKBA member.

Elegance in Twickenham

Huntsville Museum of Art's 2010 Decorator Showhouse

Suzanne Richard Barnes of Richard & Company Interior Design

Jeff White Photography

The Master Bath had consisted of a small bath off the dressing room and a hall bath. The wall between was removed and the magic began. As you step into the space, you will immediately notice the arched topped antiqued mirror set in stone that echoes the pattern of the vaulted mahogany ceiling. The chandeliers distinguish the separate areas of the bath, which is further emphasized with intricate stonework on the floor and walls. More than 1000 pieces of beveled and hand cut stone create the pattern in the center of the bathroom.

The vanities that were original to the house once boasted the unique legs on the medicine cabinets. We separated the legs from the vanities and reused the marble tops, adding in new fixtures. The legs now make the base for the fabulous custom antiqued glass mirror medicine cabinets.

A swoosh of drapery and a light shading sheer soften the retreat, creating a true mixture of the old and the new.

Special Purpose Spaces

Venetian Fantasy

Kips Bay Showhouse
James Rixner of James Rixner Interiors
Photographer: Nick Johnson

This grand reception room on the parlor floor of an Upper East Side town house was treated as a salon by James Rixner for the Kips Bay Decorator Showhouse in 2003. The feature wall was upholstered in three icy shades of Chase Erwin Silk. Couture craftsmanship was used to create the individually sewn, upholstered and hand tufted harlequin patterned design which forms the backdrop for a collection of vintage pieces. The dramatic turn of the century oil paintings of Venice were highlighted with projectors hidden in the ceiling. James' custom designed sofa spreads its arms to welcome the visitor. A rare Art Deco Aubussan rug from F.J. Hakimian anchors the space with its dramatic star designs. The twenties mirrored cocktail table and mirrored cabinet from Andre Arbus are from Malmaison Antiques, NYC.

Artist Loft

Historic Ellicott City's Decorator Show House

Dee Cunningham of Deelite Design

These children stayed perfectly still throughout the entire showhouse event. They are tromp l'oeil imagery created by artist Dee Cunningham, who painted other faux finishes, including those that grace salvaged furniture gems displayed in this artist's loft.

Fashion Studio

33rd Bucks County Designer House & Gardens
Kerry Udinski Interiors
Kim Billingsley Photography

Modern and rustic accents are juxtaposed for a sophisticated, elegant workspace full of creativity.

Rhapsody in Blue

34th Bucks County Designer House & Gardens
Kimberly Lux of Lux Interiors
Kim Billingsley Photography

A bygone era of sophistication is evoked with a music room, where an artist's sky helps spirits soar.

Shimmering Salon

Kips Bay Decorator Showhouse
Charles Pavarini III Design Associates, Inc.

Designed to relax the spirit and stimulate the mind, this room is part Piano Lounge, part Social Lounge. The ambience gives a nod to the past while taking you on a trip to the future. The room has three different areas and was designed as a lounge – one that you could find in a space residentially, and you could also find it in a boutique hotel. It's focal points include a Steinway hand-carved piano by John Eric Byers, a 'floating' fireplace in mother of pearl with birch logs, a luminous iceberg photograph, and a stunning couch that updates an 1890s tête-à-tête with contemporary, clean lines.

BALENCIAGA

Night Club

RNS Showhouse at the Shore

Michelle and Bill Collins at Painted River Studios

Photography by John Armich

The perfect getaway for friends right at home, this extensive lounge area features a wet bar, fireside chat center, and a gaming table. Stainless steel brings modernity to a timeless brick surround.

Mirror Image

Millenium Showhouse 2000
Ho Sang Shin of Antine Shin, LLC
Marisa Pelligrini Photographer

Perfect symmetry characterizes a withdrawing room, where a double lounge chair and ottoman allow flex seating for intimate groups by the fire.

Prescription for Respite

34th Bucks County Designer House & Garden
Rebecca Bancroft, Christine Edmonds, & Meg Newell of trove décor llc
Kim Billingsley Photography

The home's history as a doctor's office and apothecary inspired this mix of vintage and modern elements in a space engineered to engender a sense of calm reflection and revival.

Conservatory Right

Stately Homes by the Sea
Luis Acevedo Interior Design
Photography by Wing Wong

A plain box of a room is transformed with a trellis ceiling suspended six inches below the actual ceiling, which was painted with a beautiful blue sky. Tangerine walls offset the sage green glaze on woodwork, while wicker and ironwork furnishings reinforce the conservatory theme.

Tuscan Sun

32nd Bucks County Designer House & Gardens
Kelly White and Arlene Stachel of Mt. Lake Pool & Patio
Kim Billingsley Photography

The beauty of outdoors blends with the warmth of relaxing furnishings in a Tuscan-inspired patio area half indoors, half out.

Exterior Backyard Patio

Sandpiper's Holiday Homes Tour
Sarah Barnard Design
Photographers: Lone Pine Pictures; Sarah Barnard

Weathered teak chairs and an antique log table provide an ideal setting to sit and enjoy the fountain. This garden path leads from the main house to a guest cottage.

Black in Back

Montclair Showhouse
Tere Bresin of Beret Designs Group, Inc.
Photography by Marisa Pelligrini

Black makes blondes and Japanned reds pop in a room with striking highlights amidst a warm beige background. Squares carry the subtle theme, in a sectional divider, a collection of wood blocks in the corner display cabinet, and turned harlequin style on the honeyed entertainment cabinet.

That's Entertainment

RNS Showhouse

Michele and Bill Collins, Painted River Studios

Photography by John Armich

Instantly you will feel that this room is as comfortable as it is grand. Imagine settling in on down-filled furniture while choosing from one of over 7000 CD's that line the shelves, or maybe just watching a movie.

Commander's Nest

Mansions in May

Nina Karamallis and the Design Team of British Home Emporium

Photography by Marisa Pelligrini

This is the room in which the Lady of the house manages the affairs of the household. This is also a room for creativity and relaxation, containing a craft center, gift wrap station, computer, and a media center.

Game Room

34th Bucks County Designer House & Gardens
Kelly White of Mt. Lake Pool & Patio
Kim Billingsley Photography

Wood and wicker are blended into a warm and inviting setting for those gathering to play.

Old Town Tavern

34th Bucks County Designer House & Gardens
Chance Worthington, Steve Shagen, & Damian Ford of Worthington Custom Builder, Inc.
Kim Billingsley Photography

Photos and posters of legendary athletes and classic sports memorabilia create a sporting atmosphere for an at-home pub perfect for the man of the house and his best buds.

Master Suites

Shanghai Room

Southwest Florida Symphony Show House
Kira Krümm Interior Design
Randall Perry Photography

The magnificent international city of Shanghai inspired the ethereal, coastal feel of this master suite, combining urban sophistication and artistic creativity. Upright wardrobe chests create a symmetrical wall display, interspersed by soft-box lighting.

Cool Ablutions

Southwest Florida Symphony Show House
Kira Krümm Interior Design
Randall Perry Photography

Soft shades of white are contrasted by silver, bronze, and pewter, with a strong focus on duality between soft, textured, organic elements and hard, clean lined architectural materials.

Master Bedroom

Sandpiper's Holiday Homes Tour
Sarah Barnard Design
Photographer: Scott Van Dyke

A classic Mediterranean boudoir styled with natural textiles, such as linen, wool, and silk. A custom walnut mantle accents the natural travertine surround of the Master Bedroom fireplace.

Master Bath Vanity

Sandpiper's Holiday Homes Tour
Sarah Barnard Design
Photographer: Scott Van Dyke

Custom cabinetry with a painstaking hand distressed finish and antique urn and long stem roses complete the look.

Master Suite

Atwood-Riley House, Designer Show House

Charlotte Iseldyke, IIDA, ASID, IACC-NA Associate, The COLOR Company

This Master Suite is overflowing with comfort and luxury. Rich patterns combining exquisite deep blues, warm raspberry, and cheerful buttery textures were inspired by the original 1827 French chandelier. A hand painted ceiling mural surrounding the chandelier further enhances the fresh French inspired details. The addition of bold crown molding balances the high ceilings of this stately home. Dressing the windows with a dreamy translucent window design allows sunlight to filter onto the elegantly appointed bedding and warms the artful reading corner. At night there is complete privacy. This Master Suite offers the ultimate invitation for solitude, rest, and reflection away from everyday cares. It beckons, "Come in and dream a while."

Open Opulence

Designer Showhouse of New Jersey
Luis Acevedo Interior Design
Photography by Marisa Pelligrini

Mirrored screens in the corner reflect the opulence of space enjoyed by a master suite. A marble fireplace warms the windowed walls and a seating area, while four posters stake out the sleeping space beneath a paneled ceiling.

Jeweled Setting

Alabama ASID

Betsy Keller, ASID, of Red Door Interiors

Photography by Jeff White

A bed bejeweled with tonal textiles commands a beautiful bank of windows and the inherent view. The suede-finished lilac walls repeat in the master bath, along with the neutral ivory tones that make the entire suite shimmer.

Swanky Slumber

RNS Showhouse at the Shore
Joseph C. Tenaglia Jr. of Joseph Design
Photography by John Armich

Inspired by the fact that Frank Sinatra frequently slept in this suite, this renovation became a combination of mid-century styling and current day practicality. The calming tones of blue and green, custom furniture using exotic woods, and wallpapers laden with organic elements of stone, gravel, and string help define both sleeping and conversational areas. The "Infinity Forest" is a unique concept used to expand the perception of the space using lighting, mirrors, and rose-of-sharon branches.

Out of the Blue

RNS Showhouse
Michele and Bill Collins, Painted River Studios
Photographer: Michael Collins

A family suite where vacationing parents can lay down, shut their eyes, and open themselves up to dreams. The children are occupied in their own private attic play space with custom sleeping beds below.

Suite Serenity

32nd Bucks County Designer House & Gardens
Tracie Dunn & Laura Owen of Home Chic Home
Kim Billingsley Photography

Black and white, crisply tailored and accented with exotic jewel tones, this suite is welcoming to guests. Exotic elements create a "world-away" feeling, and the necessary luxuries are present to pamper and indulge guests in an environment reminiscent of boutique hotels.

Dreaming in Color

Museums of Old York Designer Show House
Nicole Yee of NY Interiors
Photography by James R. Salomon

Black and white set the tone for colorful dreams in a sun-flooded suite with a balcony and view as its focal point.

Contributors

Designers

Alice Shanahan Interiors
Berkeley Heights, New Jersey
908-898-0700

All the Trimmings
New Hope, Pennsylvania
215-794-8211

Antine Shin, LLC
Fort Lee, New Jersey
www.antineshin.com

Ashley Moos Interiors
Summit, New Jersey
908-273-2283

Audra Kennedy Designs LLC
Huntsville, Alabama
www.audrakennedydesigns.com

Barbara Ostrom Associates
Mahwah, New Jersey
http://www.barbaraostromassociates.com

Becoming Home Design
Flemington, New Jersey
908-256-4663

Beret Design Group, Inc.
Upper Montclair, New Jersey
www.beretdesigngroup.com

Boehm Graham Interior Design
Bedford, New Hampshire
617-692-0400

British Home Emporium
Madison, New Jersey
www.britishhomeemporium.com

Byford & Mills
Little Silver, New Jersey
www.byfordandmills.com

Canterbury Design Kitchen Interiors
Morristown, New Jersey
www.canterburydesign.com

Carrie Leskowitz Interiors
Fort Washington, Pennsylvania
www.carrieleskowitzinteriors.com

Charles Pavarini III Design Associates, Inc.
New York City
www.pavarinidesign.com

Chris' Cottage
Doylestown, Pennsylvania
www.chriscottage.com

Cica Lisa Designs
New Hope, Pennsylvania
www.cicalisadesigns.com

The COLOR Company
Huntsville, Alabama
www.thecolorco.com

C.R. Interior Designs
Short Hills, New Jersey
www.caitlinrutkay.com

Creative Interiors
New Providence, New Jersey
www.creativewallcoverings.com

Deelite Design LLC
www.deelitedesign.com
410-707-9246

Doylestown Kitchen and Decorating Studio, LLC
Doylestown, Pennsylvania
267-880-6452

Enchantment Lives
Summit, New Jersey
www.enchantmentlives.com

European Country Kitchens
Millburn, New Jersey
www.eckitchens.com

European Home Collection, Inc.
Buckingham, Pennsylvania
www.EuropeanHomeCollection.com

Gass Design
Doylestown, Pennsylvania
www.gassdesign.com

George Bond Interior Designs
Newcastle-upon-Tyne, United Kingdom
http://georgebond.tv

Gracious Living Home Furnishings
Lahaska, Pennsylvania
www.graciousinteriors.com

Hendrixson's Furniture
Furlong, Pennsylvania
www.Hendrixsonsfurniture.com

Home Chic Home
Chalfont, Pennsylvania
www.homechichomedesigns.com

Hunting and Gatherings
New Hope, Pennsylvania
www.huntingandgatherings.com

Joan L. Curtis, Designer & Muralist
Newtown, Pennsylvania
215-598-8058

Jonathan Hress
Bedminster, New Jersey
908-470-0713

Joseph Design, LLC
Wildwood Crest, New Jersey
www.JosephDesignLLC.com

Kelley Price Interiors
Chalfont, Pennsylvania
www.kelleypriceinteriors.com

Kerry Udinski Interiors
Doylestown, Pennsylvania
215-348-7307

Kira Krümm Interior Design
Estero, Florida
www.kirakrumm.com

Le Blue Goose
Skippack, Pennsylvania
www.lebluegoose.com

Luis Acevedo Interior Design
Leonia, New Jersey
www.luisacevedointeriors.com

Lux Interiors
Richboro, Pennsylvania
www.LuxInteriors.com

Lycknell Interiors
Wyomissing, Pennsylvania
http://www.gloriastewardlycknell.com/

Mark Pettegrow Studio, Ltd.
Point Pleasant, Pennsylvania
www.pettegrowstudio.com

Minion-Gutierrez
New York City
www.miniongutierrez.com

Mt. Lake Pool & Patio
Doylestown, Pennsylvania
www.mt-lake.com

NICHE
Encinitas, California
www.design-niche.com

NY Interiors
Oakland, California
www.nicoleyee.com

Painted River Studios
Corbin City, New Jersey
www.paintedriverstudios.com

Papyrus Home Design
Boonton, New Jersey
www.papyrushomedesign.com

Phillip Greenberg Interiors
East Norriton, Pennsylvania
www.phillipgreenberg.com

Pierre Deux French Country
Ardmore, Pennsylvania
www.pierredeux.com

Red Door Interiors
Huntsville, Alabama
www.reddoorinteriors.biz

Richard & Company Interior Design
Big Cove, Alabama
www.RichCoInteriors.com

Sarah Barnard Design
Los Angeles, CA
www.sarahbarnard.com

Shannon Hall Designs
Charleston, South Carolina
www.shannonhalldesigns.com

Sheila Rich Interiors, LLC
Monmouth Beach, New Jersey
www.sheilarichinteriors.com

Superior Woodcraft
Doylestown, Pennsylvania
www.superiorwoodcraft.com

trove décor llc
Newtown, Pennsylvania
www.trovedecor.com

Tuscan Hills, LLC
Kingston, New Jersey
www.tuscanhills.com

Umphrey Interiors
Birmingham, Alabama
www.umphreyinteriors.com

Village Flower Shoppe, Ltd.
Haute House Interiors
Lahaska, Pennsylvania
215-794-5900

Worthington Custom Builder, Inc.
New Hope, Pennsylvania
www.worthingtoncustombuilder.com

Showhouses

Alabama ASID

www.asidal.com

The Alabama Chapter of the American Society of Interior Designers has teamed up with The Women's Guild of the Huntsville Museum of Art to present decorator events that benefited both the museum and the ASID chapter.

Atwood-Riley Designer Showhouse

This stately home was known as the Atwood-Riley House at the time of this Designer Showhouse. Located in the Twickenham Historic District of National Registry Structures, this home provided the first location for Huntsville, Alabama's current private Randolph School. The front door once read, "No Admittance Yankees!" and still exists with faint writing in its new location in the basement. It was owned by, among others, a congressman, a tailor, and a plantation owner.

Birmingham Home & Garden Loft Tour

www.literacy-council.org

This decade-old annual event in Birmingham, Alabama, benefits the Literacy Council Tour. The council works to provide literacy services throughout Central Alabama.

Birmingham Symphony Decorator Showhouse

www.symphonyvolunteercouncil.org

Members of the former Junior Women's Committee and the former Women's Committee of the symphony initiated this event in 1976.

Bucks County Designer House & Gardens

www.buckscountydesignerhouse.org

This annual event benefits Doylestown Hospital and the Mission of the Village Improvement Association of Doylestown. It has been a gala event in the Philadelphia suburbs since the early 1970s, operating annually since 1978.

Designer Showhouse of New Jersey

www.humcfoundation.com

This annual spring event benefits the Hackensack University Medical Center Foundation, and features the work of designers and landscapers from the Garden State and New York City.

DogHause

www.pspca.org

This four-week, annual fall event transforms historic properties in the Philadelphia region into showcases for gala events. Top designers participate in the effort to create an event that raises funds to find homes for animals in need.

Kips Bay Decorator Showhouse
www.kipsbay.org
For almost four decades, this annual, premier decorator event has been launched to benefit the Kips Bay Boys and Girls Club located in the Southeast Bronx, New York. For over ninety-two years, Kips Bay has played a critical role in helping to shape the lives of thousands of young children throughout the New York metropolitan area.

Historic Ellicott City, Inc. Decorator Show Houses
www.historicec.com
This annual event benefits the organization that works to restore and preserve this historic Maryland town and to promote education, entertainment, and enrichment to the community and its many visitors.

Junior League of Montgomery Showhouse
www.jlmontgomery.org
This women's organization promotes voluntarism, developing the potential of women and improving the community through the effective action and leadership of trained volunteers. Its purpose is exclusively educational and charitable.

Madame Walker Showhouse
The home of Madame C.J. Walker, the nation's first African American Millionaire, was home to a decorator showhouse in November 1998 to benefit the United Negro College Fund.

Mansions in May
www.wammh.com
This event takes place every other year and is sponsored by the Women's Association of Morristown Memorial Hospital to raise funds for specific hospital projects. The month-long event is run by over 1,000 volunteers and attracts approximately 18,000 visitors.

Museums of Old York Designer Show House
www.oldyork.org
The Museums of Old York was founded more than one hundred years ago to preserve the history and artifacts of York, Maine, one of New England's earliest colonial settlements and the nation's first incorporated city (1642). With nine historic museum buildings, the organization showcases early art, architecture, and decorative arts and focuses on the stories of southern Maine's men, women, and children. The showhouse has been an annual fundraiser for more than two decades.
Contact: Erica A. Holthausen, Museums of Old York, P.O. Box 312, York, ME 03909; (207) 363-4974; development@oldyork.org

RNS Showhouse at the Shore
www.rnscancerandheartfund.org
This annual summer event has been staged by the Ruth Newman Shapiro Cancer & Heart Fund for nearly two decades. The proceeds benefit area hospitals, including AtlantiCare, Shore Memorial Hospital, Cape Regional Hospital, and Bacharach Institute for Rehabilation.
Contact: Terry Calvi (tcalvi@hotmail.com)

Southwest Florida Symphony Show House
www.swflso.org/symsociety.html
This symphony's supporters, in the form of the Symphony Society, stages gala showhouse events in order to support the organization first founded as a community orchestra in 1961. The organization shares its gift of music with the region's communities through a number of programs and concerts.

Stately Homes by the Sea
www.statelyhomesbythesea.com
Founded in 1912, Visiting Nurse Association of Central New Jersey is the largest voluntary, nonprofit home care agency in New Jersey, serving more than 100,000 individuals each year in Monmouth, Middlesex, and Ocean Counties. The proceeds from the annual showhouse event are used to benefit home care, hospice, and other community-based services and programs.

Susan G. Komen Holiday House Designer Show House
www.komennyc.org
This new annual event in New York City pools design talent to create gala events that funnel funds toward one of the nation's most successful grassroots causes, the fight against breast cancer.

Twin Maples Showhouse
historictwinmaples.org
The Fortnightly Club, together with the Overlook Hospital Auxiliary and the Summit Junior Fortnightly Club, were very proud to present the Twin Maples Centennial Show House in 2008, celebrating the Estate's 2nd Century of Service to our many area charities. The Fortnightly Club, founded in 1893, purchased the Twin Maples Estate as its headquarters in 1949, restoring the property in 2007. In 2008, thanks to the help of 45 talented interior and landscape designers, many builders and architects, countless tradesman and volunteers hours, Twin Maples was transformed during a benefit for The Carol G. Simon Cancer Center at Overlook Hospital and the Twin Maples Historic Preservation Fund.

Vassar Showhouse & Gardens

www.vassarshowhouse.org

In 2006 the 40th anniversary of the Vassar Show House took place at Willowbrook Farm, dating from 1873. The farm includes a large farmhouse, Pennsylvania bank barn, spring house, and other supporting structures. Over 30 interior and landscape areas were designed for the showhouse. The showhouse benefitted the Vassar Club scholarship fund.

Women's Guild of the Huntsville Museum of Art

www.hsvmuseum.org

Created in conjunction with the Alabama Chapter of the American Society of Interior Designers, the guild organized a designer showhouse in September 2005 to raise funds for the art museum. The event was held at Harris Hill Farm near Huntsville.

Photographers

Ann Stratton Studio, Inc.
New York, New York

Brad Nicol

Charlie Daniels

Daniel Eifert

David Groul

Greg West

James J. Salomon

Jeff White

Jeffrey J. Hanshaw
J. Hanshaw Photography, Inc.

Jim LaBranche

John Martinelli

Joy Levy

Kim Billingsley
www.kimbillingsley.com
215-353-1313

Lone Pine Pictures

Marisa Pelligrini
www.marisapellegrini.com
646-296-7762

McKay Imaging

Melinda and Hal Kuehne

Michael Collins

Nick Johnson

Peter Paige

Peter Rymwid
973-628-1527
www.peterrymwid.com

Photography by John Armich
www.johnarmich.com
215-262-8015

Randall Perry

Renee Fox

Scott Van Dyke

Sylvia Martin Photography
www.sylviamartinphoto.com
205-422-6969

Terry Welch Photography
Concord, New Hampshire

Top Kat Photo
Katrina Mojzesz
www.topkatphoto.com
877-401-5652

Wing Wong, Memories TTL, LLC
Rutherford, New Jersey
www.memoriesttl.com

Other Schiffer Books by Jeffrey B. Snyder
Antique Majolica Around the House. ISBN: 076432134X. $49.95
Art Glass Today. ISBN: 9780764334641. $50.00
Art Jewelry Today 2. ISBN: 9780764330650. $50.00
Ceramics Today. ISBN: 9780764334658. $50.00
Ironwork Today 2. ISBN: 9780764330643. $50.00
Printmakers Today. ISBN: 9780764334627. $50.00
Wood Art Today 2. ISBN: 9780764334634. $50.00

Other Schiffer Books on Related Subjects
Showhouses 1: A Decorators' Tour.
Tina Skinner. ISBN: 9780764332722. $44.99
Showhouse Review: An Exposé of Interior Decorating Events.
Tina Skinner. ISBN: 9780764328640. $44.95

Dedication

To Tina Skinner, who developed this book series and had much to do with the early stages of this second edition. Your inspirations and insights are much appreciated.

Schiffer Books are available at special discounts for bulk purchases for sales promotions or premiums. Special editions, including personalized covers, corporate imprints, and excerpts can be created in large quantities for special needs. For more information contact the publisher:

Published by Schiffer Publishing Ltd.
4880 Lower Valley Road
Atglen, PA 19310
Phone: (610) 593-1777; Fax: (610) 593-2002
E-mail: Info@schifferbooks.com

For the largest selection of fine reference books on this and related subjects, please visit our web site at **www.schifferbooks.com**
We are always looking for people to write books on new and related subjects. If you have an idea for a book please contact us at the above address.

This book may be purchased from the publisher.
Include $5.00 for shipping.
Please try your bookstore first.
You may write for a free catalog.

In Europe, Schiffer books are distributed by
Bushwood Books
6 Marksbury Ave.
Kew Gardens
Surrey TW9 4JF England
Phone: 44 (0) 20 8392 8585; Fax: 44 (0) 20 8392 9876
E-mail: info@bushwoodbooks.co.uk
Website: www.bushwoodbooks.co.uk

Library of Congress Control Number: 2010941009

Designed by RoS
Type set in BernhardMod BT/Humanist521 BT

ISBN: 978-0-7643-3649-2

Printed in China

SHOW

HOUSES

2

A Decorators' Tour

Jeffrey B. Snyder

Schiffer Publishing Ltd
4880 Lower Valley Road · Atglen, Pennsylvania 19310